Martial Arts

Marshall Cavendish
Benchmark
New York

This edition first published in 2010 in North America by Marshall Cavendish Benchmark

Marshall Cavendish Benchmark
99 White Plains Road
Tarrytown, NY 10591
www.marshallcavendish.us

Published in 2009 by Evans Publishing Ltd, 2A Portman Mansions, Chiltern St, London W1U 6NR

© Evans Brothers Limited 2009

Editor: Nicola Edwards
Designer: D.R. Ink
All photographs by Wishlist Images except for page 6 Jung Yeon-Je/AFP/Getty Images; page 8 Kazuhiro Nogi/AFP/Getty Images; page 14 Sam Yeh/AFP/Getty Images; page 15 Shaun Botterill/Getty Images; page 18 Paul Gilham/Getty Images for DAGOC; page 21 Jung Yeon-Je/AFP/Getty Images; page 22 Alexander Blotnitsky/AFP/Getty Images; page 26 Vladimir Rys/Bongarts/Getty Images; page 27 Toshifumi Kitamura/AFP/Getty Images

Library of Congress Cataloging-in-Publication Data

Gifford, Clive.
  Martial arts/by Clive Gifford.
      p. cm. — (Tell me about sports)
  Includes index.
  Summary: "An introduction to martial arts, including techniques, rules, and the training regimen of professional athletes in the sport"—Provided by publisher.
  ISBN 978-0-7614-4457-2
  1. Martial arts—Juvenile literature. I. Title.
  GV1101.35.G54 2010
  796.81—dc22

                                2008055993

Printed in China.
135642

Contents

Tell Me About . . .

Martial Arts	6
Throws and Blows	8
Martial Arts Clothing	10
Schools and Teachers	12
Martial Arts Stars	14
Judo	16
Karate	18
Tae Kwon Do	20
Kickboxing	22
Kung Fu	24
The World of Martial Arts	26
Where Next?	28
Martial Arts Words	29
Index	30

Martial Arts

▲
Top martial artists test their skills in competitions and tournaments. Here, a referee watches a contest at the 2008 Tae Kwon Do Invitational Tournament in China.

The word *martial* means "to do with war" and martial arts are ways of fighting and training to fight. Some of the first martial arts were designed to kill or harm opponents. Others were invented to help people defend themselves from attackers. This is called self-defense.

Most of the martial arts began in Asia. During the twentieth century, many martial arts teachers left Asia and began teaching in America and Europe. Today, millions of people all over the world take part in martial arts. They enjoy challenging themselves with different moves, in both training and competition.

Every martial art has its own style and rules. Some martial arts, such as karate and kickboxing, are split into many different styles. These are called schools or systems. The martial art of kung fu has more than 400 different schools.

One of the great things about most martial arts is that you can start learning them at any age. There are beginning classes for all age groups.

Once you get into a martial art, you may never stop! Thousands of people stick with martial arts all their lives. As well as being fun to perform, they can help you get really fit and give you confidence.

▼ A group of young karate students in action. Learning new moves with others is lots of fun.

Throws and Blows

Some people practice martial arts for fun and do not enter competitions. Many others enjoy competing. Contests in competitions are usually between two people. Referees and judges watch and keep score. The contestants score points for good moves, such as an accurate kick or a fast, controlled throw.

▼ Judo throws can be spectacular, as Ilias Iliadis of Greece proves. He's on top as he throws his Japanese opponent, Hiroshi Izumi, to the floor.

▲ Three young martial artists practice a kick to the front. Their teacher looks on to correct any errors.

Judo is a popular type of grappling martial art. This means that a competitor tries to throw his or her opponent to the floor. Then, he or she tries to hold or pin the opponent to the floor to win points.

Tae kwon do is a striking sport. This means that it involves kicking and punching. There is no wrestling or holding in tae kwon do. In fact, points are taken off your score if you grab your opponent or throw him or her to the ground.

Kickboxing is a striking sport in which the speed and power of kicks and punches are important. You must also avoid and defend against your opponent's attacks.

Martial Arts Clothing

Most martial arts are performed in bare feet. Each martial art has its own uniform. In karate, you wear a thin cotton jacket and pants called a *gi*. In tae kwon do, you wear a similar white outfit called a *dobok*. A judo outfit is called a *judogi*. It is thicker and looser than the karate jacket. This is because judo involves wrestling and grabbing hold of your opponent's jacket.

Most martial arts uniforms come with a belt or sash. These are colored to indicate your rank or grade in the martial art.

▼ A martial arts teacher will show you how to wear your clothing and tie your belt.

The Highest Grades

A tenth **dan**, or degree, black belt is the highest rank possible in karate. Japan's Hirokazu Kanazawa is the only tenth-dan black belt in the world!

A black belt in judo isn't the highest possible grade. A red-and-white belt is awarded to someone who reaches a grade above black belt.

As you learn more and improve, you will change belts. Most of the time you will only compete against someone with the same color belt as you.

Everyone who takes part in a martial art has to take safety very seriously. Kickboxers, for example, wrap their hands with a long roll of material that looks like a big bandage. This helps protect them from injuries.

When fighting against someone else in kickboxing and other martial arts, you have to wear lots of safety gear, including a helmet. In tae kwon do, for example, you wear a helmet, a padded trunk protector, and padded guards on your arms, your lower legs, and around your groin.

▲ This kickboxer is using a handwrap to protect his hands. Handwraps are wrapped around the hand, knuckles, and wrist.

▼ This martial artist is ready for action. She wears a jacket, a belt, padded gloves, and a headguard.

Schools and Teachers

Martial arts are not sports you can learn at home or from friends. You need to go to regular classes and practice sessions. These are held at schools, sports clubs, and gyms. In many martial arts, the place where you learn the martial art is called a **dojo**.

Each dojo has different rules and ways in which the classes are run. However, all dojos insist that you show respect to everyone else there, especially the martial arts teacher. He or she is often called *Sensei*.

Your martial arts teacher will take you through a warm-up. This prepares your mind and body for training. The

▶
These two young martial artists bow to each other before they start sparring. Bowing is a sign of respect in martial arts.

teacher will then show you new moves and have you practice and improve the moves that you already know.

When you practice your moves against another person this is called **sparring**. Sparring is a good way of improving your skills. You never have to spar against an opponent unless you want to.

▲ Many moves are practiced in groups. Everyone follows the movements of the teacher.

Your teacher may give you some exercises for you to do at home. But apart from these, you should never use your martial arts skills outside of your class.

▼ Each move in martial arts has to be performed perfectly. Here, a teacher adjusts one student's stance.

Martial Arts Stars

A handful of top martial artists find work in movies helping with stunts. Some, such as Chuck Norris, Jean-Claude van Damme, and Jackie Chan, become major film stars.

However, most martial arts champions are not wealthy or famous outside their sport. They practice martial arts because they love

▼ Two members of Taiwan's women's judo team perform a practice bout in front of their coach (*left*).

▲ Mexico's Guillermo Perez celebrates winning an Olympic gold medal in tae kwon do. He defeated Yulis Gabriel Mercedes of the Dominican Republic.

the sport and they push themselves to be as good as they possibly can. Some champions become respected teachers and open schools to train new martial artists.

To become a martial arts champion takes a huge amount of training. Champions have to dedicate themselves to their sport. They train and practice every day and eat very healthily.

Before training, champions stretch their bodies. Stretching prevents injury and improves flexibility so they can bend their bodies in all directions. Martial artists may also prepare their minds by meditating. This relaxes them and helps them focus on the competition or training session ahead.

Judo

Judo means "gentle way" in Japanese. It is a wrestling-style martial art that developed out of another martial art called ju-jitsu. People who perform judo are called **judoka**.

Judoka use timing and skill rather than force to throw their opponents to the ground. In judo you use the force of your opponent's movement against him or her. This means that smaller judoka can still win fights, called **bouts**. It also makes judo a great martial art to learn for self-defense.

A judo bout takes place on a mat called a *tatami*. Bouts for adults are usually 5 minutes long for men and 4 minutes long for women. Junior bouts vary in time.

The Scoring System in Judo

The two most important types of points scored during a judo bout are *ippon* and *waza-ari*. You are awarded *ippon* if you perform a perfect throw that lands your opponent on his or her back. This wins you the bout.

You can also be awarded *ippon* if you hold your opponent on the mat for a long period of time or if he or she gives up by banging on the mat twice. This is called **submission**.

Waza-ari is half an *ippon*. You are awarded *waza-ari* if you make a good, but not perfect, throw or manage to hold your opponent on the mat for a shorter time. Scoring two *waza-ari* wins you the bout.

▲ These two judoka are in the middle of a bout. They hold on to each other's jackets and look for a chance to strike.

▲ The female judoka uses her right foot to sweep her opponent's leg away. She hopes to unbalance him so that she can throw him.

In judo you can grab hold of your opponent's jacket as you wrestle for an advantage. You try to throw your opponent over your shoulder, hip, or leg onto the mat. Once on the mat, you try to hold or pin down your opponent to score points.

A referee walks around the mat. To interrupt a bout, the referee calls, "Matte." Then the two judoka must move away from each other.

▲ The referee signals that a hold on the mat has been successful. *Ippon* is scored and the judoka on top has won the bout.

Karate

Karate means "empty hand" in Japanese. It is a martial art that was designed for self-defense. No weapons are used. Karate began on islands off the coast of Japan. People who learn karate are called **karateka**.

There are three different parts of karate. *Kihon* is practicing the basic techniques, such as your **stance** (how you stand) and the most common kicks, punches, and defensive movements. Defensive moves are called *uke*. These use parts of the hand or arm to block an opponent's punch or kick.

▶

The karateka on the left uses his left hand and arm to block an attack from his opponent. At the same time, he strikes his opponent's body with his right hand.

18

Kata are short patterns of movement involving punches, steps, kicks, and other moves. There are over 100 *kata*. Karate students practice groups of *kata* in a row, similar to a dance.

▲ This karateka is performing a *mae geri*: a front kick in which the lower part of the leg is snapped forward.

Kumite is the third part of karate and it involves sparring with an opponent. Karate bouts are usually short, but the action is intense. In most competitions, judges award points when one karateka completes a good move. If one karateka gets eight points ahead, the bout stops and he or she is the winner.

◄ Taiwan's Chen Yen Hui aims a high kick at her opponent during the 2006 Asian Games. Karate has been part of the Asian Games since 1994.

Tae Kwon Do

Tae kwon do is the national sport of South Korea. *Kyorugi* is the sparring form of tae kwon do. People in more than 130 countries take part in tae kwon do. It is an Olympic sport, too.

The action in tae kwon do bouts is fast and furious. You have to stay balanced and on your feet as you avoid your opponent's punches and kicks.

A tae kwon do bout usually lasts for three rounds. The bout takes place on a mat that is 40 feet (12 m) square. Points are awarded by three judges. To score a point, you have to strike one of the target areas on your

▶

Two young martial artists practice their tae kwon do moves. The boy in red tries to make a fist strike but is struck in the stomach with a side kick by his opponent.

opponent's body with your foot or fist. The target areas are the head and the front and sides of the body.

Since your legs are longer and more powerful than your arms, most of the moves that score points are kicks. These include spectacular moves like jumping side kicks: you fly through the air, turn your body, and strike with your heel or sole of your foot.

Tae Kwon Do

Steven Lopez of the United States became the first person to win two Olympic gold medals in tae kwon do. He won the lightweight division at the 2000 and 2004 games.

If you pretend to be injured in a bout to get a rest, you can lose half a point from your score. This is called a *kyong-go*.

In 1956 Korean tae kwon do teacher Jhoon Rhee arrived in America with less than fifty dollars in his pocket. He would go on to teach tae kwon do to thousands of people, including Bruce Lee and Muhammad Ali.

▼ Bineta Diedhiou of Senegal makes a spectacular high kick to her opponent's head. In Olympic competition, a clean strike to the head or neck with the foot is worth two points.

▼ You must wear a padded trunk protector when sparring with others. The red parts of the protector show the scoring areas.

Kickboxing

Kickboxing grew out of other martial arts, such as karate and tae kwon do. It is a mixture of regular boxing, kicks, and **blocks**.

There are many forms of kickboxing, including **Muay Thai**. This is Thailand's national sport and is very difficult. Boxing gloves are the only protection that Muay Thai fighters wear. Fighters are allowed to strike with their elbows and knees as well as their hands and feet.

Other types of kickboxing are less dangerous. Semi-contact kickboxing allows only punches and kicks, which have to be above the waist.

▼ Champion kickboxer Anatoly Nasyrev (*left*) blocks a kick with his right arm while striking with a left-handed punch.

You can practice your kicks and punches on a large punching bag. This kickboxer is performing a straight jab punch.

Focus mitts are padded blocks held by a kickboxing coach. They provide you with a moving target at which to aim your kicks and punches.

Kickboxers often practice their stance and their movements in front of a full-length mirror.

Kickboxers use punches that come from boxing. These include the jab, which is the most common punch. Kickboxers learn ways of blocking punches and kicks. They also bob and weave out of reach of an opponent's attack.

There are many different kicking moves. To do an ax kick, you lift your leg up very high and then chop it down, like an ax. Skilled kickboxers try to deliver a punch and a kick one right after the other. This is called a **combination**.

Some kickboxers never spar with a real opponent. Instead, they practice their moves on pads and punching bags for exercise and for fun.

▼ These two young kickboxers both attempt an attack. The boxer to the left performs a jab punch. The boxer to the right attempts a powerful **roundhouse kick**.

Kung Fu

Kung fu is a Chinese martial art that is many centuries old. There are many different schools of kung fu.

Kung fu clothing is different from clothing worn in other martial arts. It is often black, although colors thought to be lucky in China, such as red and yellow, are also worn. Instead of being loose and tied with a belt, as in judo and karate, kung fu outfits button up at the front.

Kung fu has dozens of moves. Some are throws and holds similar to those in other martial arts, but many other moves are copied from the movements of creatures in nature. You strike quickly, like a snake, and shape your hand like a tiger's claw.

▼ These young martial artists are learning kung fu. The teacher (*center*) demonstrates a pose that they are supposed to copy.

▲

There are many different stances to learn in kung fu. Most are named after real or pretend creatures. This is the dragon stance.

▲

The crane bird is said to represent patience and grace. People adopting the crane technique try to keep their opponents at a distance before striking.

▲

The leopard is all about speed. People fighting leopard style aim to attack with short, sharp moves.

Tai chi is a form of kung fu. It is mostly practiced as a series of slow, flowing movements. Tai chi is used as daily exercise by tens of millions of Chinese people.

▶

A teenager practices a kung fu move in front of the Olympic Stadium in Beijing.

Kung Fu

The Epo Kung Fu School in Dengfeng, China, has 6,800 students. It is one of 80 kung fu schools in and around Dengfeng.

In 2008 Disney released the animated film *Kung Fu Panda*. Animators used some real kung fu moves when drawing the training and fighting scenes.

The World of Martial Arts

Martial arts competitions are held all over the world. Many games, such as the Asian Games and the Pan-American Games, feature a range of sports and include some martial arts. Karate, for example, first appeared in the Pan-American Games in 1995.

Two martial arts are Olympic sports. Judo first appeared in 1964. Tae kwon do was demonstrated at the 1988 Olympics and became a full sport (in which players compete for medals) in 2000.

▶

A karate bout at the 2007 Pan-Arab Games, which took place in Cairo, Egypt.

In most competitions the competitors are divided into different weight groups. This means that you don't have to be tall or huge to be successful at martial arts. Ryoko Tani is only 4 feet 9½ inches (1.46 m) tall, yet she has won an amazing seven World Championships and two Olympic gold medals in judo.

Karate's biggest competition is the World Championships.

These were first held in 1970. They are now held every two years, each time in a different country. The 2010 competition will be held in Belgrade, Serbia.

Kickboxing has many different organizations that hold competitions. This can mean that there are dozens of world champions at one time. Like boxers, kickboxers often fight in single bouts, rather than competing in a championship.

▼ Judo star Ryoko Tani throws Frederique Jossinet to the ground during the 2004 Olympics. Tani won a gold medal to add to her seven World Championships.

Where Next?

These websites and books will help you find out more about martial arts.

Websites

http://www.theshotokanway.com/
There is lots of information on karate at this website, including advice and tips for beginners.

http://www.wtf.org/
The home page of the World Tae Kwon Do Federation is a very useful site. It explains some of the basics of tae kwon do. It also lists major competitions.

http://www.judoinfo.com
There is plenty to read and learn at this website about judo training and moves. There are useful links to other websites, too.

http://www.wkausa.com
The official website of the World Kickboxing Association USA. It provides rules, competition results, a list of kickboxing clubs, and links to other websites.

http://www.karateworld.org/
This website for the World Karate Federation, the largest karate organization.

http://www.ijf.org
The International Judo Federation website has a hall of fame for champions, results of competitions, and tips on many of judo's most common moves.

Books

Levigne, Heather. *Martial Arts in Action* (Sports in Action). New York: Crabtree Publishing, 2003.

Martial Arts Words

blocks Moves used to stop an opponent's punch or kick from striking the intended target area.

bout A contest between two people in most martial arts.

combination A series of punches and kicks that are thrown one right after the other.

dan A level of ability, or grade, in many martial arts.

dojo The place where people learn and practice many martial arts.

judoka A person who practices judo.

karateka A person who practices karate.

Muay Thai Also known as Thai boxing, this is kickboxing where knees, elbows, and low kicks are allowed during a bout.

roundhouse kick A martial arts move in which you swing your foot and leg up and around in a half circle to strike your target.

sparring Training by fighting with another person. Martial artists usually wear full protective clothing and headgear for sparring.

stance The way you stand and position your body during martial arts movements.

submission Giving up in a martial arts bout because you cannot move or are in pain. Usually, a submission means you lose the contest.

Index

Numbers in **bold** refer to pictures.

Asia, 6

belts, 10, 11, 24
blocking, 18, 22, 23
bouts, 16, 17, 19, 20, **26**, 27
boxing, 22, 23

Chan, Jackie, 14
Chinese, 24
clothing, 10, **10**, 11, **11**, 24
combination, 23
competitions, 6, 8, 19, 26, 27

defense, 18, **18**
dojo, 12

flexibility, 15

holding, 9, 17, **17**, 24

Japanese, 16, 18
judges, 8, 19, 20
judo, 8, **8**, 10, 16, 17, **17**, 24, 27
ju-jitzu, 16

Kanazawa, Hirokazu, 11
karate, 7, 10, 18, **18**, 19, **19**, 22, 24, 26, 27
kickboxing, 7, 9, 22, **22**, 23, **23**, 27
kicks, 8, 9, 18, 19, **19**, 20, **20**, 21, **21**, 22, **22**, 23
kung fu, 7, 24, **24**, 25, **25**

mat, 16, 17, 20
meditating, 15

Norris, Chuck, 14

Olympic Games, 20, 21, 27
opponents, 6, 9, 10, 13, 16, 17, 18, 19, 20, 23

protection, 10, **10**, 11, **11**, **21**, 22
punches, 8, 9, 18, 19, 20, 22, **22**, 23, **23**

referees, 8, 17
respect, 12, **12**, 15
rules, 7, 12

safety, 10, 11
scoring, 8, 9, 16, 17, 19, 20, 21
self-defense, 6, 16, 18
South Korea, 20
sparring, 13, 19, 20, 23
stance, **13**, 18
steps, 19
stretching, 15
submission, 16

tae kwon do, 9, 10, 11, 15, 22, 27
tai chi, 25
Tani, Ryoko, 27, **27**
teachers, 6, 12, 13, **13**, 14, 15
Thailand, 22
throws, 8, 9, 16, 17, 24, **27**
timing, 16
training, 6, 12, 13, 15

van Damme, Jean-Claude, 14

warm-up, 12
wrestling, 9, 16, 17